AIRCRAFT CARRIERS

by Matt Doeden

Lerner Publications Company • Minneapolis

Lerner Publications Company
A division of Lerner Publishing Group
241 First Avenue North
Minneapolis, MN 55401 USA

Website address: www.lernerbooks.com

Words in **bold type** are explained in a glossary on page 30.

Library of Congress Cataloging-in-Publication Data

Doeden, Matt.
    Aircraft carriers / by Matt Doeden.
      p. cm. – (Pull ahead books)
    Includes index.
    ISBN-13: 978-0-8225-2666-7 (lib. bdg. : alk. paper)
    ISBN-10: 0-8225-2666-2 (lib. bdg. : alk. paper)
    1. Aircraft carriers–Juvenile literature. I. Title. II. Series.
V874.D64 2006
623.825'5–dc22   2005001205

Manufactured in the United States of America
1 2 3 4 5 6 – JR – 11 10 09 08 07 06

Whoosh! Where did that airplane
come from?

It came from an aircraft carrier. Aircraft carriers are warships. They are like airports on the ocean.

Aircraft carriers carry airplanes all around the world. How do airplanes take off from aircraft carriers?

Aircraft carriers have long **flight decks**.
Flight decks are like runways at airports.

Airplanes need to go very fast to take off. How do airplanes on aircraft carriers get going so fast?

Strong **catapults** help airplanes gain
speed to take off. A catapult acts like
a big slingshot.

Airplanes are going very fast when they land on aircraft carriers. How do they stop?

Sailors stretch long **arresting wires** across the flight deck.

Airplanes catch the arresting wires to slow down.

Who is in charge of an aircraft carrier?

The captain is in charge. The captain
tells the other sailors what to do.

The captain watches what is happening from the bridge.

The bridge is a room inside the **control tower.** Sailors steer an aircraft carrier from the bridge.

The control tower rises high above
the flight deck. What is below the
flight deck?

The **hangar bay** is below the flight
deck. Airplanes are stored in the
hangar bay.

Sailors fix and clean airplanes in the hangar bay.

There are more rooms below the
hangar bay. Sailors sleep in some
of these rooms.

Sailors also eat in a room below the hangar bay.

Aircraft carriers have huge engines.

The engines make power to turn the
propellers. The propellers push the
aircraft carrier through the water.

Aircraft carriers
are not fast.
How do
they protect
themselves?

Aircraft carriers have guns. But
they are not built for fighting up
close. Aircraft carriers need help
from other warships.

Aircraft carriers usually sail in
battle groups. Battle groups have
many warships.

Warships in battle groups stay close.
They protect each other.

Aircraft carriers are important ships.
They are like floating airports!

Facts about Aircraft Carriers

- The U.S. Navy's *Nimitz*-class aircraft carriers are the largest warships in the world. Each one is longer than three football fields!

- The USS *Lexington* was the first U.S. Navy aircraft carrier to be destroyed in battle. Torpedoes sank the *Lexington* during World War II.

- A large aircraft carrier can carry more than 3,000 sailors.

- Each *Nimitz*-class aircraft carrier costs about $4.5 billion to build.

- Many U.S. Navy aircraft carriers are named after important people in United States history. For example, the USS *George Washington* is named after the first president of the United States.

Parts of an Aircraft Carrier

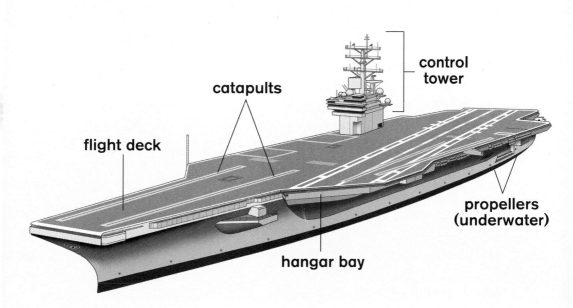

catapults

control
tower

flight deck

propellers
(underwater)

hangar bay

Glossary

arresting wires: wires on the decks of aircraft carriers that airplanes catch when they land. Arresting wires help slow airplanes.

catapults: machines that help airplanes take off from aircraft carriers. Catapults act like big slingshots.

control tower: parts of aircraft carriers that rise high above the flight deck

flight decks: long, flat areas on top of aircraft carriers

hangar bay: the area on an aircraft carrier where airplanes are cleaned and fixed

propellers: spinning blades that push aircraft carriers through the water

Index

About the Author

Matt Doeden is a freelance author and editor living in Minnesota. He has written and edited hundreds of children's books, including more than a dozen military titles.

Photo Acknowledgments

The photographs in this book appear courtesy of: U.S. Navy photos provided by Navy Visual News Service, Washington, D.C., cover, pp. 3, 4, 5, 6, 7, 8, 9, 10, 11, 12, 13, 14, 15, 16, 17, 18, 19, 20, 21, 23, 24, 25, 26, 27, 31; © Koichi Kamoshida/Stringer/Getty Images, p. 22. Illustration on p. 29 by Laura Westlund, © Lerner Publications Company.